To Sophie & Daisy
Love from Grandma

Hoki
the story of a kakapo

Hoki
the story of a kakapo

Gideon Climo & Alison Ballance

Line drawings by Jo Ogier

A WILD SOUTH BOOK

To our special friends Ruth and Calypso

Thanks to the following for their help with the book: Arno Gasteiger; Ferne Mackenzie of the Department of Conservation; Don Merton; Rod Morris; Michael Stedman; Kennedy Warne and the Auckland Zoo. The authors would particularly like to acknowledge Dave and Joy Crouchley and the Paton family from Maud Island for all their support and encouragement.

All photographs are by Gideon Climo, with the exception of the following:
pp. 7, 25, 39, 52, Arno Gasteiger; 9, Don Merton; 10, 12, 13, 14 (left), Department of Conservation; 8, 48, Rod Morris; 11, 14 (right), Auckland Zoo.

Wild South is a trademark of Television New Zealand Ltd

Published by Godwit Publishing Limited
15 Rawene Road, P.O. Box 34–683
Birkenhead, Auckland, New Zealand

First published 1997

© 1997 Gideon Climo & Alison Ballance (text);
Gideon Climo (photographs except those credited otherwise); Jo Ogier (line illustrations)

ISBN 1 86962 009 7

Cover and page design by Shelley Watson
Production by Mirella Monteiro
Printed in Hong Kong

Contents

Foreword, Don Merton   6

Introduction, Alison Ballance   8

1. A Troubled Beginning   10

2. Hoki's New Home   15

3. A Roof Over Her Head   21

4. A Bright Spark   26

5. What's on the Menu?   31

6. A Fragrant Heavyweight   40

7. The Company of Friends   47

8. Hoki's Christmas Present   53

To Find Out More About Kakapo   60

Foreword

'ONE OF THE MOST WONDERFUL, perhaps of all living birds' is how Dr Sclater of the British Museum in London described the kakapo when the first specimens reached Europe. One hundred and fifty years on, Sclater's sentiment remains undisputed, for as we learn more about the kakapo's behaviour, physiology and bizarre life-style — fashioned over millions of years in the isolation of primeval New Zealand — we cannot help but conclude that the kakapo is indeed a remarkable bird and a very special element of New Zealand's natural heritage — our 'taonga' or living treasure.

The kakapo is now one of the world's rarest and most critically endangered birds. By the mid-1990s only fifty kakapo were known to survive — nineteen females and thirty-one males. And between 1986 and 1996 only three kakapo chicks hatched and survived — two males on Little Barrier Island and one female, Hoki.

Kakapo are now biological refugees in their own land, and we surely have a moral obligation to do our very best to reverse their seemingly unstoppable slide to extinction. The Department of Conservation, Comalco and the Royal New Zealand Forest and Bird Protection Society are totally committed to saving the kakapo, and I believe the species is finally poised for recovery. As I write this (on Codfish Island in February 1997), the kakapo are breeding and hopes for a successful season are high!

Throughout her five years in captivity on Maud Island Hoki has been cared for by Gideon Climo, Kakapo Programme Officer based on Maud Island. Gideon is to be congratulated on his remarkable achievement, as never before has a kakapo been maintained in captivity for so long. Hoki is the only kakapo in the world that is comfortable in the close proximity of people, and her scientific, educational, breeding and advocacy potential is thus unique.

I applaud Gideon Climo and Alison Ballance, not only for their considerable personal contributions to kakapo conservation, but in particular for giving us all this unique insight into the character and personality of Hoki — in my view one of the most wonderful of all living birds!

Don Merton. QSM, (hon) DSc
Codfish Island
24 February 1997

Introduction

FOR A WELL-KNOWN BIRD, there is a lot that is not known about the kakapo. Despite the huge effort that goes into managing them, even the most basic questions such as 'How long do they live?' are still unanswered. Although every one of the fifty kakapo alive today has a name, most of them go for months without being seen by a human. The kakapo workers who spend months in the field monitoring them do so at a distance, using radio tracking and automatic scanners so the birds are left as undisturbed as possible.

There is one kakapo, however, who is well used to people. This bird is Hoki — and she offers insights into kakapo behaviour that are both universal to her species and unique to her.

The person who is most familiar with Hoki is Gideon Climo, who, since the middle of 1992, has had the major responsibility for looking after her. Although other people have also been involved in Hoki's care, she and Gideon have a very special relationship, and he is the only person since the naturalist Richard Henry in the late 1800s who has had the opportunity to get close to kakapo and observe them on their own terms.

I met Gideon and Hoki when I began working on a 'Wild South' television documentary on kakapo, and I was struck both by Hoki's engaging personality and by Gideon's enthusiasm and commitment. He enthralled me with stories of watching Hoki grow up, and I was sure that everyone with an interest in New Zealand's unique natural heritage would be equally fascinated.

As part of his programme of caring for Hoki, Gideon keeps a daily diary in which he records her behaviour and the events in her life. These diaries offer a wonderfully intimate portrait of a kakapo's life, and Gideon and I decided to collaborate so that we could share with others some of the magic revealed in their pages. What follows is a blend of diary excerpts and Gideon's recollections, which allow us to share with him the fascination of getting to know a kakapo.

Alison Ballance
TVNZ Natural History
Dunedin, 1997

Chapter 1

A Troubled Beginning

HOKI'S LIFE GOT OFF to a rocky start. She was one of a handful of chicks born on Codfish Island in the autumn of 1992, a year that began full of promise for kakapo but ended in disappointment. It was the first time the thirty kakapo on the island had tried to breed since they were transferred there from Stewart Island between 1987 and 1991, and the breeding season began well.

The rimu trees on Codfish Island were covered in green fruit that, as it ripened through the autumn, should have provided an important food supply for the kakapo. But in March the island was lashed by strong storms, and the rimu fruit remained green. The five nesting females were spending most of the night away from their nests foraging, and the chicks were beginning to starve.

Something had to be done urgently, so in early April Don Merton and other Department of Conservation staff began the job of finding nests and rescuing the chicks. Two starving chicks were sent to Auckland Zoo to be hand-reared,

Kakapo breed only once every two to four years. Female kakapo are solo mothers, raising chicks on their own without any help from the male. The female selects a nest site, usually a cavity inside a rotten tree or under a rock and then prepares a soft, deep layer of litter by chewing and shredding dry wood. She lays one to four small white eggs — about the size of pigeons' eggs — which she then incubates for thirty days. Once the helpless chicks have hatched, the female will feed them for up to six months, often walking more than 4 kilometres in a night to collect food for them.

and a third was fostered with another Codfish Island female, Nora, who had been incubating infertile eggs. The kakapo team was busy putting out food such as apples and kumara to entice the females to feed, but the birds showed little interest.

By early May, Nora's foster chick was beginning to lose condition and it too had to be rescued, to join the other two female chicks — Alf and BJ — at Auckland Zoo. The starving chick was given royal treatment on her plane flight north — her own Business Class seat. The third chick had been nicknamed Gale — after her grandmother, Nora, the north wind, and her mother, Zephyr, a gentle breeze — but she was given the official name of Hoki, meaning 'to return', a name chosen from a national competition in schools run by the

Kakapo Recovery Programme sponsor, Comalco.

After sixteen days of being kept in isolation at the zoo because of the possible danger of infection, Hoki was introduced to the two other chicks, including her sister BJ. Zoo curator Mick Sibley was worried about how the birds might react to each other, but he needn't have been concerned. Alf was busy eating her first ripe coprosma berries; BJ at first ignored the newcomer, but within a few minutes she and Hoki were nuzzling each other happily.

By early June the chicks' grey down had been replaced by their first proper feathers, and they were putting on weight. They were playful but clumsy, 'purring' loudly when they were expecting food.

Suddenly first Alf and then BJ sickened and died.

Autopsies showed that they had both suffered acute respiratory problems caused by the inhalation of food particles.

Hoki, however, continued to thrive, and three weeks later, when she was three months old, she made the second big plane journey of her life, to Maud Island in the Marlborough Sounds.

Maud Island was already home to five wild kakapo — two females and three males — and a special aviary had been built and planted with trees and shrubs to provide food and shelter. It was to be the beginning of a new, settled chapter in what had so far been a rather turbulent life.

Chapter 2

Hoki's New Home

HOKI ARRIVED ON Maud Island in the middle of winter, on 6 July 1992. It was lunchtime when she was released, so she was greeted with a gourmet banquet of kakapo delights, including grapes and pear, kumara and broccoli, nuts and honeywater. She took a couple of bites from an offered grape before slowly wandering away from her travel box. As she went she gently pulled at pieces of grass and leaf litter, testing them with her beak, much as young children examine and taste objects by putting them in their mouths.

After ten minutes she reached the end of the enclosure and settled down to sleep with her head tucked over her right shoulder. Half an hour later she woke and began moving around, eventually wandering into the darkened shelter, where she slept for the rest of the afternoon.

By dusk Hoki was awake again and she headed over to the feeding platform to check out the offerings. She tasted everything but couldn't seem to decide what she wanted to

eat. Eventually she went off to check out her new surroundings, biting everything around her. She was fascinated by leaves, constantly picking up and dropping different types.

Although she had been kept under twenty-four hour light at the zoo and had been active both day and night, it didn't take her long to adjust to behaving like a wild kakapo, sleeping during the day and being active in the darkness.

For the first two weeks we kept Hoki under constant observation from a little room to one side of the enclosure behind a pane of glass. After dark we used a night-vision scope to see what was happening. Hoki seemed aware of our presence there and would occasionally wander over to tap at the glass with her beak and peer through, making 'blowfishes' at us the way small children do at a window.

A daily routine soon became established. Fresh food was brought in at night and the old food cleared away during the day. Hoki was weighed daily to keep a check on her condition and health. She was quite happy to be handled and treated being put on the electronic scales almost as a game. Sometimes I got her to weigh herself by putting pieces of food in places that she could reach only by standing on the scales.

Hoki was very talkative, keeping up an almost constant chatter of grunts both to herself and to me when I was near her. If she had been in the wild, she would still have been with her mother

and nest mates, although they would have left the nest and moved further afield. She seemed to regard me, by now the most familiar person in her life, as her surrogate mother.

Her confidence and co-ordination were improving rapidly. On the first night she had played around at the bottom of a sloping ponga log, but after ten days she was happily climbing to the very top, pausing to stretch her wings and feet on the way up.

After two weeks in the pen she was showing a lot of interest in what was on the other side of the metre-high partition that separated the smallest inner pen from the other two areas making up the rest of the enclosure. After three weeks, when I opened up the partition leading into the middle pen, Hoki moved straight through into the new space, exploring a tangle of logs and branches and biting at the bark. Within minutes she was rushing around, giving everything a quick once-over. She returned to me — the one familiar object in this new place — and then moved off again more slowly. She climbed up a log, flapping her wings madly to maintain her balance, and then descended to carry on her exploration.

After her first night in the larger pen I found her

roosting out in the open with no cover above her. I tried to entice her into a new roost box but she didn't want to enter, so in the end I led her to a natural roost under a clump of toetoe. I left her roosting with just her head hidden and her body sticking out, but a shower of rain soon caused her to retreat to her usual place in the inner area. A very wet and windy night soon after this was the first time that I had really seen Hoki in the rain. Although she was soaked, she looked very calm and comfortable.

Hoki's moods changed from day to day. Although she was mostly quiet and placid, she could sometimes be boisterous and playful, even rough. At times she would just sit next to me when I was in the pen at night, enjoying my company, occasionally climbing up on to my shoulder and gently chewing and nibbling around my ear. At other times, though, I called her 'the green racer', as she rushed madly around, pulling at my gumboots and demanding playful rough and tumble.

I was interested to see how much her tail had grown since she arrived. Although she was fully feathered, she didn't have full adult plumage; that wouldn't develop until after her first moult the following year. Her young feathers were smaller and more closely matted than her adult feathers would be, and the speckled patterning was denser and more intense.

I continued to feed her in the usual place. She had now been weaned off the infant formula that had been a staple part of her zoo diet and was eating a mixture of parrot pellets,

---

Birds that fly have strong, stiff feathers to help them stay airborne, but because kakapo don't fly their feathers are very soft. Like most birds, kakapo oil their feathers to keep them waterproof, and even on very wet days the fine down below the outer feathers will be dry and effective insulation.

Kakapo's faces are framed by stiff, whiskery feathers, which give them a very owl-like appearance — hence their name 'owl parrot'. The function of these whiskers is not known.

nuts, fruits and vegetables, essentially the same as the supplementary diet that had been developed for the wild kakapo.

At the end of July I noticed, to my surprise, that Hoki had eaten — in fact chewed — one of the five-finger seedlings that I had planted in the pen. She had pulled branchlets off, eaten the ends of the stalks and peeled the bark off. It was just like the feeding signs that wild kakapo leave, although somewhat messier.

By late August Hoki had destroyed all the plantings in the middle pen, and I decided it was time to let her out into the much larger outside pen. She had already been displaying a strong interest in this area, scaling a ponga tree by the wall and peering over at me as I worked in there at night, getting the pen ready for her. When I opened the door Hoki didn't pause for a second. She took one quick look through the door and ran in, flapping her wings and jumping. She headed off around the pen, giving it the same sort of rapid inspection that she always gave a new place, nipping at plants as she passed, before returning to where I was sitting writing up my kakapo diary. She sat on my boot for a while, taking the leaves off clover plants, and then climbed on to the diary, tugging at the pen and at the pages of the book. She eventually climbed on to my shoulder. It was a nice feeling — a kakapo enjoying the company of a friend. Hoki was settling in well to her new home.

Chapter 3

A Roof Over Her Head

HOKI HAS A CHOICE of places to roost in: artificial wooden structures that I have built, as well as natural roosts I have provided and some that she has created for herself. Sometimes she simply perches in dense cover up in the trees or in long grass on the ground. One of her favourite roosts is a large nikau palm frond, the bulb of which makes an ideal waterproof roof under which she can hide.

When Hoki first arrived on Maud Island I was concerned about the way she roosted, hiding only part of her body and leaving the rest exposed. By the time she was living in the big pen, however, she seemed to have worked out how to hide herself properly and had become very wary about revealing herself during the day. She sometimes changes roosts, but only if she can stay under cover and not expose herself in the open areas of the pen. Even at dusk she stays in the bush or along its fringes, not venturing into the open until it is properly dark.

Hoki often favours a particular roost for a few days, or

even a few weeks, before choosing somewhere else. She keeps her roosts tidy, defecating in one corner. Occasionally she even cleans it out, kicking the droppings outside. I clean her roosts out regularly, but I usually do this at night, as Hoki becomes very defensive during the day.

Hoki has a number of ways of showing her unease about the presence of people around her roost. One day, when I was in the pen with a visitor, she crept just outside and raised all the feathers on her shoulders and head, like a cat fluffing out its fur to make itself larger and more intimidating. She bobbed her head down, picking up a dead twig and throwing it towards us as a sign of her discomfort. We took the hint and retreated, leaving her in possession of her 'castle'.

If she is hiding in a large roost and has room to move around, she stands and raises her wings above her head until they touch at the tips, making herself look as large and threatening as she can.

Male kakapo make the same display at their track-and-bowl system if they feel threatened by an intruder, such as another kakapo or one of the burrowing seabirds that also live on the kakapo islands.

Occasionally Hoki becomes defensive about other places that she considers her own. One morning, when I was turning on the weighing system and testing its platform with my hand, she became very protective and upset. She appeared out of nowhere, rushed up on to the platform and began snapping her beak and lifting her wings at me. Then she froze, staying

> Kakapo hide themselves during the day to avoid aerial predators. In the past, this would have included birds such as the now extinct Haast's eagle and the goshawk, but now it is only harrier hawks and the occasional falcon that patrol overhead.
>
> Kakapo roosts may include a crook in some tree-top branches, the middle of a low bush or under a fallen log on the ground.

Adult male kakapo have what is known as a track-and-bowl system, which consists of one or two roughly circular depressions dug in the dirt and connected by a system of tracks. Early observers thought the depressions were dust bowls, but in the 1970s Don Merton and others realised that kakapo used them as part of their display to attract females. When he is displaying, a male kakapo inflates large air sacs on his chest, until he looks like an over-inflated football. He then emits a deep, low sound known as a boom, which can be heard over several kilometres. He also makes a high metallic call, known as chinging. Booming takes place in summer and often lasts all night, and a male may boom and ching as many as 24,000 times in one night.

very still as if she had suddenly realised it was too open and light, and that she shouldn't be there. She sat for a while before rushing back into the safety and cover of the bush.

Hoki varies her roost depending on the weather. In winter, after a few days of rain, she may climb up in the branches of a tree where she can dry out in the breeze, or she may sit in the entrance of a ground roost, basking in the warmth of the sun. Conversely, if it is too hot, she will rest

high in a tree to cool off in the breeze, or if it is a still, hot day, she may retreat into the coolness of an underground den. The wild kakapo on the island behave the same way, adjusting their roost according to the weather.

Even when she is roosting on the ground, Hoki will almost always find a root or rock to perch on and cling to with her feet, rather than sitting belly down on the dirt. She sleeps in a variety of postures — with her head dropped down on to her chest, resting across her shoulder or sometimes tucked under her wing.

During the day Hoki is often calm, peaceful and sleepy, but sleeping isn't her only daytime activity. She spends time preening and, if she is in a roost that contains plants, chewing on things around her. As soon as it becomes dark, Hoki is at her most energetic. It is as if she has to expend all the energy she has bottled up during the day. As night progresses she calms down, and by dawn she is spending most of her time feeding.

Chapter 4

A Bright Spark

KAKAPO, LIKE ALL PARROTS, are among the smartest birds in the world. It wasn't long before I was having to offer Hoki 'mind therapy' to stop her becoming bored with her enclosure.

    I have built her several adventure playgrounds, constructions of branches including a beam, a ladder and a swing. The first night she saw the 'equipment', she didn't take any notice until I went over to it, tapping it and sitting on it. She sat at a distance until I started to push the swing, then she came over and sat in front of it, moving in time with it. When she grabbed it and hopped on, I gave her a push, which she seemed to enjoy. When I was a kid with a pet budgie I never imagined that I might one day be pushing one of the world's most endangered birds on a swing!

    I then walked to the end of the beam and tapped the ladder for her to climb up, which she did. She walked right along the beam, pausing at bits she wasn't sure about but more confident if I tapped it in front of her. When I walked

away she stayed, walking back and forth along the whole log to see how to get off. She eventually found the best way: jump! As I left the pen she let out two loud, echoing skrarks — it was the first time I had ever known her to make this sound.

By the end of her first year Hoki had stopped grunting to herself and began to skrark much more, usually as I was leaving the enclosure at night.

As well as playing on the adventure playground, Hoki created her own toys and amusements. Springy branches were a particular favourite. I'd often watch as she played on a branch, balancing herself as she moved along it and jumping

Skrarking is a loud sound often made by wild kakapo. They usually skrark as they come out of their roost each evening, to let other birds know of their presence. They also skrark when they return to the roost in the morning. Male kakapo skrark a lot at the beginning of the booming season and will skrark if they are disturbed or are chasing something away from their track-and-bowl system.

at the bunch of leaves at the end until the bough gave way under her weight. Then she'd rush back up, determined to grab the branch and hold it down. She would also swing on rata vines that I strung between trees as a challenge for her sense of balance. Sometimes, too, I found myself becoming an extension of Hoki's playground as she climbed up and over me, and swung upside down, holding on to my clothes with her strong beak.

At times her play became an intelligence test for her and an amusement for me. On one particularly memorable occasion she walked down a springy branch to get off, and her weight bent the branch so that it was just touching the ground. Hoki was reluctant to jump down and have it spring from under her, sending her flying. She moved a bit closer to the end but missed her balance and ended up hanging from her feet with the tip of her beak on the ground. This was another step towards a landing so she took one of her feet off the branch and stretched it towards the ground. She now faced an even greater dilemma — if she let go, the branch would hit her on its way up. So, after much hard thinking, she lifted her foot from the ground and gripped the branch again. Pulling her body up, she clamped her beak on to the branch, and then let go with her feet. She hung by her beak for a while, with her feet just touching the ground, then released the branch, sending it springing safely back without knocking her on the way past. I was most impressed!

One morning when I was in her pen changing the food

hoppers I saw Hoki in her roost holding a piece of bark, about 30 centimetres long, in her beak. She was playing with it gently and peacefully. Holding it in one foot, she would bite at it then, with it in her beak, she would hold her head high with pride. She was trying to place it just outside the roost where I was crouching; it was as if she wanted to give it to me.

My activities in the pen often provide her with much enjoyment — at times she stares at me as if I'm a clown provided for her entertainment. My tools, especially the yellow handle on my screwdriver, are appealing to her. If she can manage to grab it, she will run off with the screwdriver and toss it about. I have noticed before that she is very attracted to yellow objects — maybe they remind her of the yellow breast of her mother.

The cord running from the weighing platform to the scales is a favourite toy. I once sat and watched Hoki as she perched, clamping the cord with her beak, heaving it up and holding the slack with her feet. She amused herself for some time trying to lift up all 5 metres of the cord, standing on all that she had stacked up under her and stretching down to take up more.

She also enjoys fiddling with the cords and zippers on my clothes and the head lamp I wear at night. I've finally realised that Hoki considers this to be part of me: she recognises me as a character with a well-known smell, voice, ways of moving — and a glowing light on the top of my head.

This was clearly illustrated one night when my lamp went out and, as I reached to turn on my hand-held torch, she fled from me. She stayed away for a while, perched in a fuchsia bush, until she had reassured herself of my identity. The batteries in the head lamp began working again, so I switched off the other torch and Hoki returned to sit by my boot. But as the batteries died again, Hoki became fearful once more and took off into the dark. On another night, as Hoki was sitting peacefully on my knee, I thought it would be nice to watch her by moonlight. As soon as I switched off the head lamp, she became scared and began biting me. It's obvious that in her eyes I am really only me when I have a light on my head.

Chapter 5

What's on the Menu?

WILD KAKAPO EAT a variety of plants, and in this respect Hoki is just like her uncaged counterparts. Although in the beginning she seemed to destroy a lot of plants without actually eating them, it wasn't long before she was supplementing her diet with food such as grasses, which were very soft and could be eaten whole.

It wasn't until late October in Hoki's first year that I saw some distinctive kakapo feeding signs, called kakapo chews. A month before that milestone I had sat and watched Hoki eating long pieces of grass the way a rabbit does — 'sucking' the grass up, her bill and cheeks moving rapidly as she chewed. Even when she was drinking water — a noisy process with much sipping and swallowing — she would make a grinding noise as if she were trying to 'mill' the water.

For the first few weeks Hoki's food was presented to her in a bowl. She seemed use her beak as a spoon to eat the parrot pellets that made up part of her diet, chasing them around in the bowl, trying to scoop them up. After she had

> Kakapo eat a wide range of vegetation, from small ground plants to parts of big forest trees, although a few species make up the bulk of their diet. They particularly like soft, new leaves and the storage parts of plants such as roots and bulbs. When trees such as rimu are fruiting, kakapo will feed almost exclusively on their fruit.

eaten most of the pellets, she would use her beak in the same spoon-like motion to sweep the crumbs into one place in the bowl so she could finish them off.

Hoki had favourite foods, which she would eat as fast as possible while ignoring the rest of the food on offer. To encourage her to eat the less-favoured food, I introduced a regime of feeding her twice each night. For the first sitting she would get the main course of pellets and vegetables, and then a couple of hours later she would be allowed the 'dessert' of walnuts and almonds. Nuts, rich in protein and fat, are also a favourite with wild kakapo.

I recorded how much of each kind of food she was eating by reweighing all the food each morning to see how much had been eaten during the night. During the first few

months, however, sparrows were making this job difficult as they would get into the food at dawn and clean up everything that Hoki hadn't eaten. In the process they also left droppings everywhere, which wasn't very hygienic. So, after a while, I put her food in hoppers, rather than in bowls.

It was easy to teach Hoki how to use a hopper as I could actually show her what to do. I held the lid open until she came over and began feeding, and then I gently lowered the lid until it was resting on her head. I also kept it wired open for a few days until she got used to it, but it wasn't long before she was quite happy lifting the lid and helping herself to food.

Until she was three months old, Hoki would feed early in the evening before heading off around the pen. Later, her pattern of activity changed, and she began to have just a snack early on, returning later in the evening for the main part of her meal.

When Hoki began showing signs of getting bored with her enclosure I incorporated her feeding routine into my efforts to introduce novelty. I placed a number of the brackets for the feeding hoppers in different locations around the pen and put food in all of them for a few days. After a couple of nights there was only one hopper that she hadn't found, so I showed her where it was. Then I began randomly varying the location of the hoppers so that each evening she had to go and search for her food. I soon realised that I would have to put the hoppers out during the day while she was roosting,

> Kakapo feeding hoppers have hinged lids that stop small birds getting in, keep rain off the food and, on Little Barrier and Codfish Islands, also stop kiore (Polynesian rats) getting at the food. Wild kakapo are trained over a few weeks to feed from hoppers. To begin with, the lids are wired open so they learn to feed from them, and they are gradually lowered. Eventually, they learn the art of eating while also propping the lid open.

otherwise she just followed me around in the evening, watching where I was placing them! I now change the position of the hoppers every month, as Hoki soon adjusts to their new locations. I try to put them in positions that will be a challenge to her, such as up a tree, so that she will have to climb to reach them.

I have continually modified how I present some of the larger food items such as kumara, apple and corn. Hoki had difficulty eating them when they were loose in a hopper as they would roll around, and she would often flick them out and proceed to play with them. This made it easy for the small birds to get at the food and meant it was often difficult for me to find the next morning. To convince Hoki to eat her food rather than play with it, I staked the kumara and apples out on pieces of wire, covering them with an upturned ice-cream container to keep the other birds off.

There were still occasions, though, when dinner became a grand game. One night I had not yet staked out her kumara and apple, which were lying on the ground near my feet. Hoki eyed them up and rushed over, jumping on them both. She grasped the kumara and apple, one in each foot, and it was as though a show had started. She tucked her head under her feet and rolled herself on to her back, still gripping both the kumara and apple. Then she rolled around and around down a slope, hanging on to her food and biting at it. She came to a halt in a dip, where she lay on her back quite comfortably for some time before beginning to eat. Dropping

Richard Henry was the first person to describe how kakapo ate. In one of his reports he wrote that 'they chew their food more effectively than any other bird I am acquainted with. For this purpose there are diagonal grooves in the upper mandible in contact with which the lower acts in the manner of a steel mill. On examining the food in their crop it is found to be so well masticated that it is impossible to tell what it is.' If the kakapo are feeding on particularly tough plants, they often just suck the juices and leave the fibrous part in a distinctive kakapo 'chew'.

the apple, she held the kumara with both feet, moving her feet closer to her head and continuing happily to eat. She seemed to be having huge fun rolling around and fighting with the food, but I also wondered if it was easier for her to eat this way, rather than holding the food with her foot while standing up.

Even when the kumara is staked out, Hoki still manages sometimes to pull it off the stake, tossing it around and playing games with it. She can also be mischievous with her feeding hoppers, pulling them out of their u-shaped brackets and strewing the nuts and seeds around. It seems that whatever refinements I introduce, Hoki soon finds a way to get around them!

One night I put out Hoki's kumara and apple near her shelter and she began feeding on the kumara straight away. She stood on it, biting pieces off to expose the white flesh. Then she bit a long, thin growth off the kumara and held it delicately in her right foot while balancing perfectly on her left. Bringing her foot up to her beak, she picked at the long growth, ignoring the rest of the kumara.

Hoki's feeding on plants in her enclosure has been useful in helping me to recognise the sorts of feeding signs that wild birds leave on different plants. At some times of the year, wild kakapo go for sweet things, mainly flax and manuka bark. It was interesting to watch Hoki the first time I put in some big flax stems, with lots of flowers and seed pods. Although I wasn't sure if she would know what to do, she was soon biting into them madly, grinding the juicy covering of the green pods and nipping the stems. She tore off a flowering pod and chewed the whole thing up before spitting all the bits out.

Ferns are one of Hoki's favourite foods, and at times she would push past me when I opened the door leading back into the middle pen, almost skipping in her enthusiastic rush to get at the ferns growing in there. The young, fresh growth of blechnum ferns and tree ferns are particular favourites. I've watched her feeding on a new branch of ponga, nibbling her way down the leaves from the tips, enjoying the lush growth. She also eats out the white flesh inside the base of ponga fronds; I have tried this myself and, although it is sticky, it has a pleasant coconut flavour.

Berries are another favoured food, especially those from coprosma bushes and five-finger trees. One night I found Hoki up in a heavily berried coprosma, gripping a fruit-covered branch with one foot, absolutely gorging herself. During one fruiting season I noticed that almost every five-finger in her pen had been climbed and fed on, and there were many clusters of berries on the ground. When I examined four droppings, they were full of berries. In one fresh dropping I counted 300 seeds; since each berry contains two seeds, that meant she had eaten 150 berries.

Although kakapo have always been thought of as strictly vegetarian, I have made a number of observations that suggest they occasionally eat invertebrates. I have found the

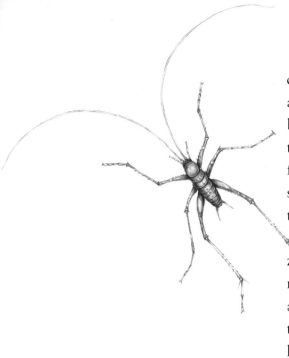

crushed remains of a pill millipede on the feeding platform, and one night I was amazed to see Hoki grab a darkling beetle that was crawling past my boot. She began immediately to crush it up while shaking her head, sending a bit of it falling to the ground. She continued to crush and then swallow what she had in her beak before looking around for the other half, which she dealt with in the same manner.

The light from my head lamp often brings moths zapping around Hoki's head and feet, and she shakes her head madly and fidgets, trying to escape them. One night she flung a moth to the ground then watched it as it wriggled about in the leaf litter. She snapped at it and, once she had the insect in her beak, she crushed it, flicking her head and swallowing the whole thing, wings and all.

The cave wetas that share some of Hoki's roosts have also come in for some attention from her. Once she disturbed some wetas, which hopped off the walls and jumped over me in panic. One foolish weta landed in front of Hoki and she snatched at it. Grabbing it in the middle, she began to grind it, shaking her head, while she ate the abdomen and the long, black legs. She lost the other half as she flicked her head about, and then immediately carried on moving about the roost as if nothing had happened.

Hoki gives me opportunities to test new kinds of foods to see how palatable they are to kakapo. In one such trial she was offered sugary foods such as raisins, sultanas, dried apricots, fresh gooseberry and coconut shreds. They were in

three different bowls, and I watched with amusement as she visited the bowl closest to her and rolled the apricots and raisins around in her beak, dropping them all again with no interest in eating them. Having checked out all the bowls, she noticed that the third container held a gooseberry, which she immediately squashed, licking up the juice and dropping the skin and flesh. The coconut shreds proved a hit, and over the next few nights she consistently sought them out. Unfortunately for Hoki, coconut was not destined to become part of her normal diet, so she had to fall back on her old favourite standby of nuts and seeds.

Chapter 6

A Fragrant Heavyweight

ONE OF THE DISTINCTIVE characteristics of kakapo is their sweet, musky fragrance, and at times this smell is quite strong in Hoki's pen. The strength of the smell varies from day to day, and the weather seems to contribute to the way it lingers; it is particularly noticeable on damp days. Although kakapo preen their feathers with oil produced from a gland at the base of their tail, the oil itself has no odour, so that is not the source of their distinctive scent.

The moss green dappled feathers of the kakapo are perfect camouflage in the forest, as I have found on numerous occasions. During the day I could be actively searching for Hoki but walk right past her, unless she moved and gave her position away. Richard Henry noticed this ability to hide — 'so well does their colour accord with the yellow and green of the ferns that it is impossible to see them unless they move.'

A kakapo's reaction to being disturbed is often to freeze, keeping absolutely still, which helps them blend in perfectly with their surroundings. One day I was cleaning out one of

> Some people compare the kakapo's sweet fragrance to old-fashioned freesias; others have described it as being a bit like a musty clarinet case. Other parrots, too, have a sweet smell, but it seems to be a particular feature that sticks in people's mind about kakapo. This characteristic makes it easy for tracking dogs to find the birds in the wild, and it probably also made them very easy for introduced mammalian predators to find.

the food hoppers, looking at the green plants in front of me and not noting anything out of the ordinary. I wandered off around the pen trying to find Hoki but couldn't see her in any of her usual roosts. I then returned to the hopper to collect something and, as I bent down, I felt as though the whole world suddenly shifted — what I had thought was a solid wall of grass and leaves moved in front of me. The whole time I had been cleaning the hopper Hoki had been sitting less than 30 centimetres away from my face and, as familiar as I was with every part of the cage, I had simply not noticed her.

If Hoki comes out during the day, she moves with exaggerated slowness and care, placing every toe on the ground as lightly as possible so as to avoid the slightest noise, which might give her away. Her head moves very little, her eyes stare right at me without blinking, and everything about her is slow and deliberate. But if she trips or gets her big toes tangled, she will suddenly break out of her 'go slow' mode and rush off, making a fool of all her efforts. She seems almost embarrassed that she has been so silly.

To me, when she is in this mode, she resembles a slow clockwork toy or a crawling bulldozer, but someone else, after watching one of these tortuous creeps, described her rather less charitably as being like an 'ancient old thing with bad arthritis'!

But Hoki is slow and quiet only some of the time. At night she can be all action, darting and zooming around like a mouse among the trees and branches, sometimes even tripping on to her face in her clumsy excitement. She skips and flaps her wings and circles around me, occasionally jumping up with both feet off the ground. She runs across my boots, sometimes stopping to climb on to my knee before she hops over on to my other leg and then jumps down before zooming off again. She can put on a very energetic performance.

Hoki occasionally displays and dances to me, although I don't know the significance of this behaviour, and I'm not sure what response she expects from me. One night in particular, Hoki climbed up a knee-high branch 4 metres away from me and, with her back to me, began bobbing her

head down and her tail up. This was all in a very slow motion, and she must have bobbed half a dozen times. The last two times she dropped her wings down by her side. I wonder what it meant.

Hoki uses her wings all the time. They help to maintain her balance when she is walking on narrow branches, she flaps them wildly to give herself some lift when she is climbing, and she uses them for extra momentum when she is running, although sometimes she just drags them along beside her. She has very strong legs; with a bit of help from her wings, she can jump from a standing position to the height of my knees.

Like all parrots, Hoki is very pigeon-toed, which makes it difficult for her to run in a straight line without veering off to one side. At times her feet tangle up beneath her or she stands on her toes and has to put her wings out to steady herself as she tips sideways. She often runs with her head held very low, and ends up digging her beak into the ground as she falls forward. On one particularly inelegant occasion, after she had come to an abrupt halt, she flung her tail up in a dramatic fan, completing her head-down, bottom-up routine.

She often climbs trees and cruises happily around in the forest canopy, gripping branches with her beak and feet. Sometimes she will descend head first from a tree, sliding her feet down above her. At other times, especially if she has to negotiate a maze of small, upward-pointing branches, she alternates between having her feet down and having her head

down, holding on with her beak, then swinging her body around and holding on with her feet, and so on.

Hoki doesn't always seem to remember that she is flightless and will launch herself out of the canopy with her wings spread, in a semi-controlled plummet to the ground. The highest I have ever seen her leap is from the top of a 4-metre tall five-finger tree, landing nearly 4 metres away. On that occasion I thought her flight was very skilled and graceful, but at other times she has the gliding skill of a brick.

Although I have only ever seen Hoki dip her feet into her water bowl, she must sometimes actually wade into her pond and bathe. I arrived at the pen one night to be met by a sodden Hoki, who was far wetter than the light rain warranted. There was a strong gusty wind, and she was walking around with her wings held high to dry in the breeze. She kept having to brace herself in the wind gusts and at one stage was blown right off her feet.

Hoki is fascinated by running water, although slightly scared by the noise it makes. When I clean out her pond she retreats to what she considers a safe distance and continues to watch the operation from there. Once, when I jokingly turned the hose on her to give her a light spray, she looked slightly perplexed but did not try to get out of the way. Another time I saw her hopping on to the ballcock arm in the pond. When her weight pushed it down and made the water start rushing in, she was unperturbed, merely taking a few sips of water before hopping off again.

When she was nearly a year old, Hoki began to lose her first set of juvenile feathers. She lost all but one of her twelve tail feathers over a seventeen-day period in late July. The last tail feather persisted for another month, dragging around after her, and the sight of a kakapo with only one feather in her tail was really rather comical. Hoki kept looking back at it as she walked, as though it were a shadow she wished would go away. New tail feathers had already started growing by the time the last worn-out feather finally fell out. During the moult Hoki often looks a scruffy old thing and not her usual dapper self at all.

The beginning of the moult coincides with the time when Hoki's weight is at its lowest ebb for the year, and this is the same for the wild birds. For male kakapo, autumn is the time when they have finished what can be as many as six months of booming, during which time they can lose up to half of their body weight. For females, the beginning of the moult often coincides with the end of a breeding season, when they have finished the most intense period of rearing chicks. Both the females and the males spend the winter eating and regaining condition and by early summer will have built up their weight to a peak again.

Hoki's lowest weight is about 1.3 kilograms and, at its maximum, it increases by up to a third, to 1.7 kilograms. Hoki is about average weight for a female kakapo, whereas larger males can be up to twice as heavy, making them the heaviest parrots in the world. There are, however, big females and small males, and body size alone is not a good guide to sexing kakapo. Although Richard Henry thought he could sex a kakapo by the length of its tail and the greenness of its feathers, the only reliable indication are freckle-like markings on the trailing edge of the outer wing feathers, which male kakapo have but which female kakapo lack.

I keep a constant watch on Hoki's weight. In the beginning she was happy to be placed on the electronic scales, but after about six months on the island she became much more independent and would not tolerate being handled, so I began to use the same scales that are used to record the weights of wild birds. The scales are in a box, and the feeding hoppers are placed in such a way that the bird has to stand on the weighing platform to reach the food.

Recently I developed a novel weighing system, although it does require some persuasion and perseverance! I suspend a small swing from a hand-held balance, and when Hoki hops on and off the swing in what she regards as a game, I can record her weight.

Chapter 7

The Company of Friends

BY THE TIME HOKI was eight months old, she was much more grown up and mature than when she had first arrived on the island. This new maturity coincided with the period when, as a wild bird, she would be becoming independent from her mother.

After six months of at least twice-daily visits, she had developed a strong trust in me and no longer felt the need to check up on me continually. After she had been living in the pen for a year, I cut back on the frequency of my visits. Although I changed the feeders every morning, I now went to the pen only once or twice a week and no longer saw her nightly.

Hoki is completely happy on her own, although she also clearly enjoys the company of people, especially the easy familiarity she has with me. However, at times she barely seems aware of me, and it is lovely to see her so independent. At other times she is eager to involve me in her activities, but I make a point of never encouraging her to play with me; I

> Once they have left their mother, when they are six to eight months old, kakapo chicks are on their own. Adult male and female kakapo are solitary and interact only at track-and-bowl systems, for a single night of courting and mating once every two to four years. Young male kakapo sometimes visit older males during the booming season, as if they are watching and learning what they should do when they, too, are old enough to boom. Occasionally a small group of kakapo will be found roosting very close to each other, and female kakapo have been found roosting next to the nest of a breeding female, as if they were making a social visit.

always let her initiate any interactions.

If she is in one of her gentle moods, she might come over to me when I enter the pen and hang around quietly, perhaps perching on my knee or climbing up on to my shoulder. At such times she often delicately chews and nibbles my ear, or tastes my face with her fat, smooth tongue. She is a pleasure to be with when she is in one of her calmer moods,

sitting on my shoulder and resting her whiskery face on mine.

When she is in one of her more hyperactive moods, though, she will cling to my fingers, nipping or biting, apparently unaware of the strength of her bill. I remember clearly the pain she managed to inflict once when she climbed up my front, trying to get on to my shoulder. She grabbed my ear, crushing and grinding it as if it were some food she was trying to mill, until I couldn't stand it any more and had to brush her off. She can also use her strong, sharp toes to good effect, kicking and raking like a cat.

For a while one of Hoki's favourite games involved clinging to the back of my gumboots as I walked around. I had to develop a special shuffle to avoid standing on her and hurting her. I did trip once as I was executing the 'kakapo gumboot shuffle', and Hoki was flung back into the grass as I fell. The only thing hurt, thankfully, was her pride — and mine! She sulked and ignored me for the rest of the night!

Hoki is able to interact with other kakapo, and the wild birds on the island will sometimes visit her or pass within skrarking distance. One evening, as I left the pen, Hoki made her usual farewell skrarks but then carried on skrarking for longer than usual. In what was her first interaction with a wild kakapo, she soon got a reply from Fuchsia, one of the females, who was very close by. Hoki skrarked loudly again, and Fuchsia called back with a long reply, sounding like a squealing pig. They both called for the next thirty-five minutes, until Hoki stopped. Fuchsia kept on calling for another half hour or so, but Hoki had begun feeding at her hopper and, although she stopped to listen each time Fuchsia called, she began to eat again when the call stopped. After a while Fuchsia gave up and moved away from the pen.

On another occasion I heard a kakapo skrarking close by. It didn't sound like any skrark I had ever heard from a female, and it turned out to be a male, Smoko. He was skrarking every minute or two, sounding quite angry and making long, drawn-out calls that sounded rather like a donkey's bray. But even when he was calling very close to Hoki's pen, she didn't reply to him. The only answers he received were squeaky mutterings from a young takahe chick roosting nearby.

On still nights Hoki can sometimes hear the males booming, but her response varies. Sometimes she stops and listens attentively, but at other times she appears oblivious to the sounds.

When I recorded her own skrarks and played them back to her, she didn't respond at all; perhaps she recognised them as her own calls and felt no need to acknowledge them. Her skrarks can, however, have a profound effect on other birds. As I left the pen one night, Hoki's farewell volley stopped a nearby blue penguin in mid-screech.

Hoki sometimes becomes the object of curiosity for other birds. One day several tui were fighting and leaping about overhead, and when Hoki crept from her

roost towards me, she kept pausing and freezing as if the tui were making too much noise. The tui were amused as Hoki sneaked along, and she became good entertainment. In fact, three came down out of the canopy to perch above her, watching her with their heads tilted down.

    I was interested to see how Hoki might react to the sight of another kakapo, so one night I took a mirror into her pen. She was very reserved and calm as she crept up to the mirror and looked at it, moving her head slowly in circles and from side to side like an owl, then running her beak along the glass. She sat for about fifteen seconds, staring at her reflection, then crept away to one side of the mirror. She paused and peeped around the side, checking the mirror again, looked away and

then checked it some more. She did this about three times before wandering off, forgetting about it all together.

One of my most enduring memories of Hoki comes from a February afternoon when a heavy hailstorm passed by. It was dark and noisy, with large hailstones pounding down and building up on the roofs and ground, and I went to the pen to see how Hoki was reacting. The pen was full of ice, and the trees were damaged by the hail, but Hoki was perched quietly on her branch in the shelter, not worried at all, just sitting in the entrance gazing out at the jumping stones of ice. When I returned later that night, the ground was still covered in soft ice. Hoki rushed around, then stopped for a taste of hailstone, which she crushed in her beak. It was odd but magical, watching a kakapo moving about with ice crunching under its feet — like seeing a bird back in the winter wilds of Fiordland.

Chapter 8

Hoki's Christmas Present

IN 1996 I BEGAN to notice subtle changes in Hoki's behaviour. Although she could be just as playful, she seemed more grown up somehow. Nobody knows at what age kakapo start breeding, but at four years it seemed as if Hoki might soon be ready. She had developed a new behaviour, a habit of nibbling gently at a finger and then beginning to pull it into her beak, while nudging my hand. Her breast would drop to the ground and she would raise her head, grunting softly. After a while her eyes would half close, and her whole body would begin to shake and shudder. She was behaving like a chick being fed by a parent, but since I had never seen it before I suspect it was a new adult behaviour rather than a hangover from her childhood. Some kinds of birds carry out courtship feeding where the male regurgitates food for the female; perhaps this was what Hoki was trying to initiate with me.

The year 1996 also saw changes in the rest of the kakapo conservation programme, including some new

neighbours for Hoki. During the winter, two kakapo from Little Barrier Island were moved to Maud Island, bringing the number there to eight. The new arrivals were a female called Flossie and a male called Richard Henry. The last surviving Fiordland kakapo, Richard Henry is a stately old gentleman who had already lived on Maud Island for a few years in the late 1970s before being moved on to Little Barrier. He settled straight back into his old patch, close to Hoki's pen. With fewer males around to compete with, Richard Henry might stand a better chance of breeding successfully and thereby keeping his Fiordland genes in the kakapo population.

Breeding is the major concern in the kakapo programme. During the last ten years only three chicks have been raised to maturity, and of those, Hoki is the only female. Although it is early days for her yet, there is a strong possibility that, as the only young female, Hoki may come to be for kakapo what Old Blue was for the black robin — the lynch-pin for the species' survival. It is vital that she is allowed to breed, and with our current level of knowledge there is no way this can happen while she remains in captivity. The only option is to let her out and allow her to mate with a wild male, so I began to prepare for that eventuality. I was excited about the idea of Hoki gaining her freedom and, I hoped, becoming a mother to more precious little kakapo, but I was slightly nervous, too. Would she take it all in her stride, as she usually did, or would she panic when she was no longer in her familiar surroundings?

> Richard Henry was one of the first people to notice that kakapo were very vulnerable to predation by introduced cats and stoats, and he made a pioneering effort to save kakapo by moving them to Resolution Island in Fiordland. But the island was within swimming distance of a stoat, and within a few years it was invaded by them. Henry's efforts, however, set a precedent that would be followed seventy years later when kakapo were first transferred from Fiordland to Maud Island. When cats began killing kakapo on Stewart Island, it was decided to find all known kakapo and move them to three offshore islands: Little Barrier, Maud and Codfish. Cats had been eradicated from Little Barrier, and possums and wekas from Codfish Island, although both islands still had populations of kiore. Although stoats occasionally swim to Maud Island, extensive trapping campaigns have always managed to remove them.

In case more stoats managed to swim from the mainland to Maud Island, Hoki's pen has been designed to be predator-proof. We wanted the pen to remain this way, but we also wanted Hoki to be able to come and go whenever she wanted. Fortunately, kakapo are about the same size as a cat, so a cat flap was the perfect solution.

I put the prototype 'Hoki door' in an inside wall, between her outer pen and the middle pen. The first night it was installed, Hoki followed me as I walked her past it. She stopped for an inspection then sat staring at the clear flap as if it were a mirror. She enjoys having a puzzle to solve and soon tapped at it with her beak. This made it sway slightly, which spooked her, so she raised her head and gave it her angry glare. I had propped the flap open a little and, even though she was scared of it, she was soon trying to squeeze through the gap to get at her favourite ferns on the other side. She tried to do it without touching anything, and it soon became obvious to her that this wouldn't work — the gap was far too small! So she stalked off and left it alone, although she kept turning back for another look, as if new thoughts about how to sneak through were popping into her head.

She had a quick rest, but it was clear that she was still thinking about this new puzzle and she came back. She sat in front of the door and, without any prompting from me, leant forward cautiously to touch it before pulling away quickly in case it moved again. She left the door and came over to where I was sitting, about 10 metres away. I then left the outer pen and went around to the middle pen to begin showing her how to use the flap and to entice her through. But just as I walked in, I heard the flap swinging, and Hoki was already standing there, as if she had appeared by magic. Once again, her intelligence and sense of adventure had helped her to solve a new problem quickly. The juicy ferns in the middle pen were her well-deserved reward.

With Hoki busy practising on the inside cat door, I began work on the real thing, which was to be installed in the outside wall of her pen. This model has a solid, rather than a see-through, door. To keep predators out, there is a weight-activated platform on the outside, which means that the door is locked until something that weighs as much as Hoki stands on the platform. Since stoats weigh much less than a kakapo, this ensures that a stoat can never get into the cage. I wanted to get Hoki accustomed to using this new door in its proper location, so I built a small holding pen around the 'Hoki door' on the outside of the pen, to make sure she couldn't escape. After her practice on the other door, Hoki readily took to using this new door — especially as she was given the added incentive of having her food hoppers put in the holding pen.

We decided to let her go in summer, when the wild kakapo might be thinking about breeding, so that even if Hoki wasn't yet ready to breed, she would still be able to have a good look around the island and familiarise herself with the other birds and new places. Kakapo seem to have a very good memory for their environment, remembering sources of food

and shelter, and Hoki would need to time to build up a mental map of the island.

Hoki's big day turned out to be Christmas Day. What a lovely coincidence! I couldn't imagine a nicer Christmas present for my friend than her freedom. During the day I removed the walls of the holding pen, and then the rest was up to Hoki. That night when she popped through the 'Hoki door', she would discover a whole new world awaiting her.

Hoki wasted no time in making the most of the opportunity. I stayed some distance away from the pen with the radio tracking equipment so my presence wouldn't distract her, and within half an hour of darkness falling I heard a very satisfying sound: the beeps of her radio transmitter were coming from a new direction — outside the pen. My mind was racing with thoughts about what she would do and what was going through her mind.

It was a busy neighbourhood that night. Three nearby kakapo were all skrarking loudly to each other, and I suspect Hoki may have been a little intimidated, for she immediately headed away from the other birds, moving rapidly north. There was nothing more I could do; I left her exploring and went home to bed.

I was out early the next morning to see where she had got to and found her back near her pen, roosting under a fallen log in the big forest. After her long walk north, she had made her way back close to where she began. I thought she might have retreated to the easy familiarity of one of her favourite roosts in the pen, but her sense of adventure was obviously still intact.

I kept putting out food hoppers for her inside the pen to give her an incentive to return. It felt strange on Boxing Day when I went to do this task — there was an emptiness about the pen that was slightly unnerving. I was used to Hoki's little green face appearing to say hello, but that day there was nothing — and nobody.

Hoki seems to be thriving on the challenges of life in the wild. She often roosts near the pen, and occasionally returns to old roosts inside the pen. She pops through the 'Hoki door' for an occasional feed and is then off outside again to continue her explorations. I don't know what the future holds for her. Even if the Maud Island kakapo don't breed during Hoki's first summer of freedom, there will always be other summers.

I'm sad in a way, as Hoki's departure is the end of a wonderful period in my life. But I have always recognised that she is essentially a wild bird, and I have refused to fall into the trap of treating her as a pet, so I'm pleased that she has won her freedom. The strongest feeling I have had for Hoki is one of great respect, and that is something I know I will never lose. It has been immensely satisfying to watch her grow up, and it will be equally rewarding to observe her progress over the next few years. Although this is an end, it is also an exciting new beginning — Hoki's adventures have really only just begun. Go well, young Hoki.

To Find Out More About Kakapo

Quest for the Kakapo, by David Butler, sets out the history of the kakapo and its conservation up until the late 1980s. Out of print, but available from libraries.

Wild South's Living Treasures of New Zealand, by Rod Morris and Peter Hayden (HarperCollins, 1995), includes a chapter about kakapo courtship.

Wild South: Saving New Zealand's Endangered Birds, by Rod Morris and Hal Smith (Random House, 1995), includes a chapter about kakapo.

Richard Henry of Resolution Island, a biography by Susanne and John Hill, looks at the life of this fascinating man. Out of print, but available from libraries.

Issue 15 of *New Zealand Geographic* (July–August 1992) contains an article by Tim Higham called 'The Kakapo of Codfish Island', which looks at the disastrous breeding season on Codfish Island when Hoki was born.

The Department of Conservation (PO Box 10420, Wellington) publishes the Kakapo Recovery Plan 1996–2005, which sets out the conservation programme for kakapo.